Teach Me... Everyday KOREAN

Volume 1

Written by Judy Mahoney
Illustrated by Patrick Girouard

Technology is changing our world. Far away exotic places have literally become neighbors. We belong to a global community and our children are becoming "global kids." Comparing and understanding different languages and cultures is more vital than ever! Additionally, learning a foreign language reinforces a child's overall education. Early childhood is the optimal time for children to learn a second language, and the Teach Me Everyday Language Series is a practical and inspiring way to teach them. Through story and song, each book and audio encourages them to listen, speak, read and write in a foreign language.

Today's "global kids" hold tomorrow's world in their hands. So when it comes to learning a new language, don't be surprised when they say, "teach me!"

All Koreans speak and write the same language. Koreans have developed several different dialects in addition to the standard used in Seoul, the capital of Korea. The dialects, except for that of Jeju-do province, are similar enough for native speakers to understand. Koreans use their own unique alphabet called Hangul, which consists of 10 vowels and 14 consonants. It can be combined to form numerous syllabic groupings. Korean words are usually spelled the way they sound. There are no capital letters. The letters making up each syllable are written together to form a square-shaped character.

Teach Me Everyday Korean
Volume One
ISBN 13: 978-1-59972-110-1
Library of Congress PCN: 2008902656

Copyright © 2008 by Teach Me Tapes, Inc.
6016 Blue Circle Drive, Minnetonka, MN 55343
www.teachmetapes.com

Book Design by Design Lab, Northfield, MN

10 9 8 7 6 5 4 3 2

INDEX & SONG LIST

다같이

우리 모두 다같이 즐겁게 노래해
우리 모두 다같이 노래하자
너의 친구 나의 친구
나의 친구 너의 친구
우리 모두 다같이 즐거웁게

The More We Get Together
The more we get together, together, together
The more we get together the happier we'll be
For your friends are my friends
And my friends are your friends
The more we get together the happier we'll be.

사

안녕하세요, 저의 이름은 영희에요. 여러분의 이름은 무엇이에요?

Hello, my name is Young-hee.
What is your name?

우리 가족이에요: 아버지, 어머니, 동생 철수, 나.

This is my family: father, mother, brother Chul-soo, and me.

동생 철수

아버지

어머니

나

My father
My brother
My mother
Me

오

내고양이. 고양이 이름은 야옹이에요. 회색의 부드러운 털을 가지고 있지요.

My cat.
Her name is Yaong-ee.
She has gray and soft hair.

고양이

내 강아지.
강아지 이름은 바둑이에요.
흰색에 검정 얼룩이
있지요.

강아지

My dog.
His name is Bahdook-ee.
He is white with black spots.

이것이 우리 집이에요.
푸른색에 갈색 지붕이 있고
노란색 꽃들이 가득한
정원이 있어요.

This is my house.
It is blue with a brown roof
and a garden full of yellow
flowers.

저의 방은 빨간색이에요. 7시에요. 일어나요! 일어나!

My room is red.
It's seven o'clock.
Get up!
Get up!

둥근해가 떴습니다

둥근해가 떴습니다 자리에서 일어나서
제일 먼저 이를 닦자
윗니 아랫니 닦자
세수할 때는 깨끗이 이쪽 저쪽 목 닦고
머리 빗고 옷을 입고
거울을 봅니다
꼭꼭 씹어 밥을 먹고
가방 메고 인사하고
유치원에 갑니다 씩씩하게 갑니다

Sun is Up
The round sun rose. Wake up!
First you brush your teeth
Brush the upper and the lower teeth
When you wash your face, wash your
    neck, this side and that side
Comb your hair, get dressed
And look at the mirror
Eat breakfast, chew thoroughly
Grab your bag and say goodbye
Go to school. Go briskly.

우리강아지

우리집 강아지는 복슬 강아지
어머니가 빨래 가면 멍멍멍
쫄랑쫄랑 따라가며 멍멍멍

우리집 강아지는 예쁜 강아지
학교 갔다 돌아오면 멍멍멍
꼬리치고 반갑다고 멍멍멍

Our Puppy
Our puppy is a plump and shaggy puppy
When mother goes to do laundry, bow-wow
Following her happily, bow-wow.

Our puppy is a pretty puppy
When I get back from school, bow-wow
Wagging its tail gladly, bow-wow.

옷을 입어요. 윗도리를 입고, 바지를 입고, 신발을 신고, 모자를 써요.

I get dressed. I put on my shirt, my pants, my shoes and my hat.

머리 어깨 무릎 발 ♪♩

머리 어깨 무릎 발 무릎 발
머리 어깨 무릎 발 무릎 발
머리 어깨 발 무릎 발
머리 어깨 무릎 귀 코 입

Head, Shoulders, Knees and Toes
Head, shoulders, knees and toes, knees and toes
Head, shoulders, knees and toes, knees and toes
Eyes and ears and mouth and nose
Head, shoulders, knees and toes, knees and toes.

For breakfast, I like to eat cereal, toast with jam and drink orange juice.

Today is Monday.
Do you know the days of the week?

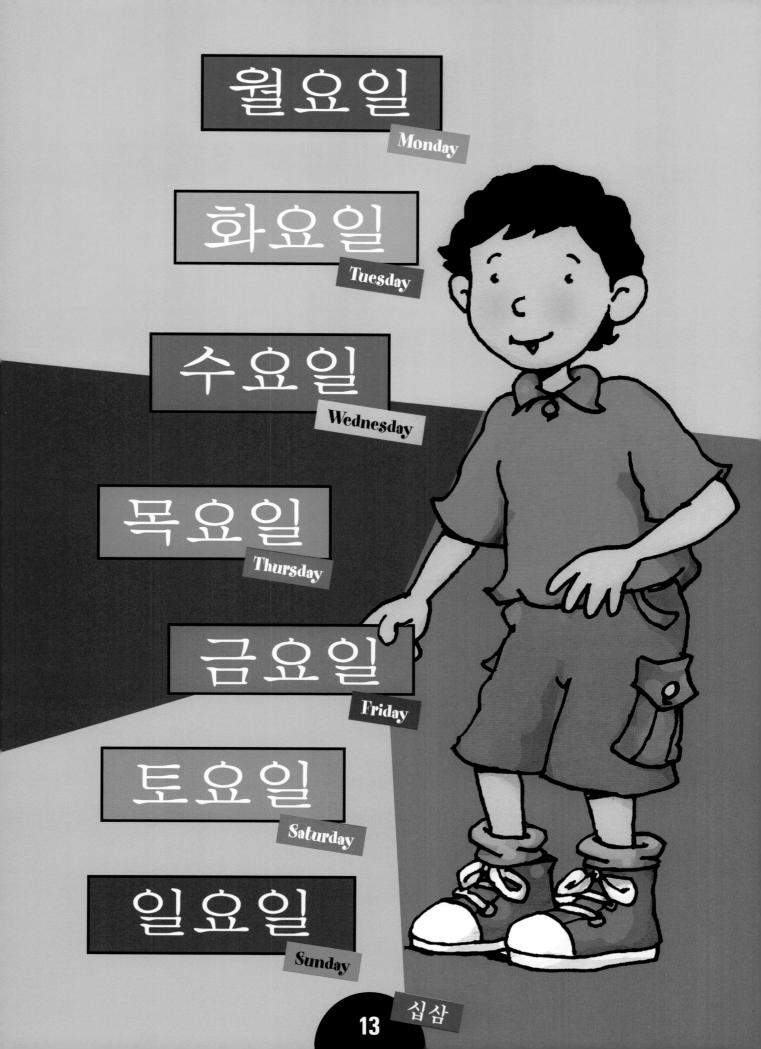

월요일
Monday

화요일
Tuesday

수요일
Wednesday

목요일
Thursday

금요일
Friday

토요일
Saturday

일요일
Sunday

13 십삼

와! 비가 와요!
날씨가 맑아지길
바래요!

Oh! It's raining!
I wish the sun would come out!

Rain Song

Silver beads hanging on a leaf of clover bush
Dangle-dangle jade bead on the cobweb
Dangle-dangle densely on each leaf
On each smiling petal 'song, song, song.'

Beautifully, thread the beads on colorful strings
Put them beside the window where the
    moonlight comes through softly
All day the beaded rain
Forms pretty beads 'sole, sole, sole.'

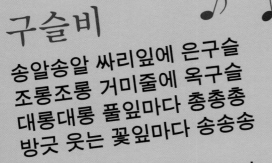

구슬비

송알송알 싸리잎에 은구슬
조롱조롱 거미줄에 옥구슬
대롱대롱 풀잎마다 총총총
방긋 웃는 꽃잎마다 송송송

고이고이 오색실에 꿰어서
달빛 새는 창문가에 두라고
포슬포슬 구슬비는 종일
예쁜 구슬 맺히면서 솔솔솔

우산

이슬비 내리는 이른 아침에
우산 셋이 나란히 걸어갑니다
파란 우산 깜장 우산
찢어진 우산
좁다란 학교길에 우산 세개가
이마를 마주대고 걸어갑니다

Umbrellas

In the early drizzling morning
Three umbrellas are walking side by side
A blue umbrella, a black umbrella
And a ragged umbrella
Three umbrellas on the narrow road to school
 Walking closely to each other.

여기가 저희 학교에요.
오늘 저는 숫자와 한글을
반복해서 공부할거에요.
저랑 같이 해보시겠어요?

저희 학교

Here is my school.
Today, I will repeat the numbers
and Korean alphabet.
Will you say them with me?

숫자

1 하나   2 둘   3 셋   4 넷   5 다섯   6 여섯   7 일곱   8 여덟   9 아홉   10 열

Numbers
one two three four five six seven eight nine ten

한글 자모

ㄱ (gi-yeok)   ㄴ (ni-eun)

ㄷ (di-geut)   ㄹ (li-eul)   ㅁ (mi-eum)   ㅂ (bi-eub)   ㅅ (si-yot)   ㅇ (i-eung)

ㅈ (ji-eut)   ㅊ (chi-eut)   ㅋ (ki-eok)   ㅌ (ti-geut)   ㅍ (pi-eub)   ㅎ (hi-eut)

ㅏ (a)   ㅑ (ya)   ㅓ (eo)   ㅕ (yeo)   ㅗ (o)   ㅛ (yo)   ㅜ (u)   ㅠ (yu)   ㅡ (eu)   ㅣ (i)

Korean Hangul Alphabet
The Hangul alphabet has 24 letters – 14 consonants and 10 vowels.
Korean words are usually spelled the way they sound. There are no capital letters.
The letters making up each syllable is made of: consonant + vowel or consonant + vowel + consonant.

열 꼬마 인디안

한 꼬마 두 꼬마 세 꼬마 인디안
네 꼬마 다섯 꼬마 여섯 꼬마 인디안
일곱 꼬마 여덟 꼬마 아홉 꼬마 인디안
열 꼬마 인디안 보이

Ten Little Indians

One little, two little, three little Indians
Four little, five little, six little Indians
Seven little, eight little, nine little Indians
Ten little Indian boys.

코끼리 한 마리

코끼리 한 마리가 거미줄에 걸렸네
신나게 그네를 탔다네
너무 너무 재밌어
다른 친구 코끼리도 불렀네

코끼리 두 마리가...
코끼리 세 마리가...
코끼리 네 마리가...
모든 코끼리가...

One Elephant

One elephant went out to play
Upon a spider's web one day
He had such enormous fun
That he called for another elephant to come.

Two...
Three...
Four...
All...

우리 모두 다같이

우리 모두 다같이 손뼉을 (짝짝)
우리 모두 다같이 손뼉을 (짝짝)
우리 모두 다같이 즐거웁게 노래해
우리 모두 다같이 손뼉을 (짝짝)

우리 모두 다같이 발 굴러 (쿵쿵)

우리 모두 다같이 웃음을 (하하)

우리 모두 다같이 맛있게 (음음)

우리 모두 다같이 낮잠을 (으음)

If You're Happy and You Know It

If you're happy and you know it, clap your
   hands (clap, clap)
If you're happy and you know it, clap your
   hands (clap, clap)
If you're happy and you know it, then your
   face will surely show it
If you're happy and you know it, clap your
   hands. (clap, clap)

If you're angry and you know it, stomp
   your feet (stomp, stomp) . . .
If you're silly and you know it, laugh out
   loud (giggle) . . .
If you're hungry and you know it, rub
   your tummy (mmm, mmm) . . .
If you're sleepy and you know it, take
   a nap (sigh) . . .

둥글게 둥글게

둥글게 둥글게 (손뼉) 둥글게 둥글게 (손뼉)
빙글 빙글 돌아가며
춤을 춥시다 (손뼉)

손뼉을 치면서 (손뼉) 노래를 부르며 (손뼉)
랄랄랄라
즐겁게 춤추자

링가 링가 링
링가 링가 링
링가 링가 링
손에 손을 잡고
모두 다함께 즐겁게 춤을 춥시다

Round, Round

Round, round (clap) round, round (clap)
Round, round turn around
And dance together. (clap)

Clap your hands (clap) sing together (clap)
La la la la
Let's dance joyfully.

Ring-gah, ring-gah, ring-gah
Ring-gah, ring-gah, ring
Ring-gah, ring-gah, ring
Hand in hand
Let's dance together joyfully.

After school, we ride home
in the car.

방과후 우리는 차를
타고 집에 가요.

자동차 바퀴

자동차의 바퀴가 데굴 데굴
데굴 데굴 데굴 데굴
자동차의 바퀴가 데굴 데굴
동네를 돌며

자동차의 경적소리 빵빵빵
빵빵빵 빵빵빵
자동차의 경적소리 빵빵빵
동네를돈다

자동차의 어린이가 밥먹자
밥먹자 밥먹자
자동차의 어린이가 밥먹자
동네를 돌며

The Wheels on the Car
The wheels on the car go round and round
Round and round, round and round
The wheels on the car go round and round
All around the town.

The horn on the car goes beep beep beep
Beep beep beep, beep beep beep
The horn on the car goes beep beep beep
All around the town.

The children in the car go, "Let's have lunch"
"Let's have lunch", "Let's have lunch"
The children in the car go, "Let's have lunch"
All around the town.

꼬마 자동차 붕붕

붕붕붕 아주 작은 자동차
꼬마 자동차가 나간다
붕붕붕 꽃향기를 맡으면
힘이 솟는 꼬마 자동차
엄마 찾아 모험 찾아
낯설은 세계여행 우리도 함께 가지요

꼬마차가 나가신다 길을 비켜라!
꼬마차가 나가신다 길을 비켜라!
랄랄랄라 랄랄랄라

귀여운 꼬마차가 친구와 함께
어렵고 험한 길 헤쳐나간다
희망과 사랑을 심어주면서 아하
신나게 달린다
귀여운 꼬마 자동차 붕붕

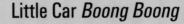

Little Car *Boong Boong*
Boong Boong Boong, a tiny car
The little car on its way
Boong Boong Boong, it smells like flowers
Which give the little car its strength
Looking for mom and adventure
Unfamiliar world, we are going together.

The little car on its way, get out of the way!
The little car on its way, get out of the way!
La la la la, la la la la.

The cute little car with its friend
Go through the rough and hard road
Giving hope and love (ah-ha)
Running happily
The cute little car, *Boong Boong*.

It is time for lunch.
After lunch, I take a quiet time.

아빠와 크레파스 ♪♪

어제 밤에 우리 아빠가 다정하신
　모습으로
한 손에는 크레파스를 사가지고 오셨어요
　음음
그릴 것은 너무 많은데 하얀 종이가 너무
　작아서
아빠 얼굴 그리고 나니 잠이 들고 말았어요
　음음
밤새 꿈나라에 아기 코끼리가 춤을 추었고
크레파스 병정들은 나뭇잎을 타고 놀았죠
　음음
어제밤엔 달빛도 아빠의 웃음처럼
나의 창에 기대어 포근히 날 재워줬어요

Dad and the Crayon
Last night, my dad, with a loving look
He bought a crayon and gave it to me
　(mm, mm)
There were lots of things to draw, but the
　white paper was too small
I fell asleep after I finished drawing my
　dad's face (mm, mm)
All night, in the dreamland a baby elephant
　was dancing
And crayon soldiers were riding leaves
　(mm, mm)
Last night's moonlight, warm like my dad's smile
Leaned on my window, waiting for me to sleep.

휴식을 취한후 저는 공원으로 놀러가요. 오리에게 먹이주는것을 좋아해요. 저는 친구와 같이 다리위에서 노래하고 춤을 춰요.

After my quiet time, I go to the park to play. I like to feed the ducks. I sing and dance on the bridge with my friends.

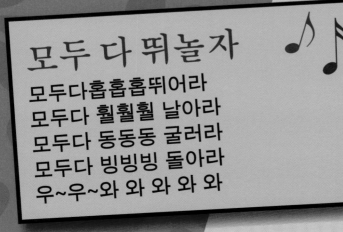

모두 다 뛰놀자 ♪♪
모두다홉홉홉뛰어라
모두다 훨훨훨 날아라
모두다 동동동 굴러라
모두다 빙빙빙 돌아라
우~우~와 와 와 와 와

Let's Play Together
Everybody hop-hop-hop jump
Everybody hirr-hirr-hirr fly
Everybody dong-dong-dong stomp
Everybody bing-bing-bing turn
Woo-woo-wha-wha-wha-wha-wha.

고기잡이

고기를 잡으러 바다로 갈까나
고기를 잡으러 강으로 갈까나
이 병에 가득히 넣어 가지고요
라라라라라 라라라라라 온다야

쏴쏴쏴 쉬쉬쉬 고기를 몰아서
어여쁜 이 병에 가득히 차면은
선생님한테로 가지고 온다야
라라라라라 라라라라라 안녕

Let's Go Fishing
Let's go to the ocean to fish
Let's go to the river to fish
Fill up this bottle
La la la la, la la la la, come back.

Sha sha sha, shi shi shi, trapping fish
When this pretty bottle is full
Take it to our teacher
La la la la, la la la la, goodbye.

배가 고파요!
저녁식사
시간인가봐요.

I am hungry!
It must be time for dinner.

오 수잔나
멀고 먼 앨라베마 나의 고향은 그곳
벤조를 메고 나는 너를 찾아 왔노라
오 수잔나 나의 노래를 부르자
멀고 먼 앨라베마 나의 고향은 그곳

Oh! Susanna
Far faraway Alabama, that's my hometown
Carrying a banjo, I came to visit you
Oh, Susanna! Let's sing my song
Far faraway Alabama, that's my hometown.

밤이에요.
여러분은 하늘의별을
바라보나요?

It's night time.
Do you see the stars in the sky?

작은별

반짝반짝 작은 별
아름답게 비치네
동쪽 하늘에서도
서쪽 하늘에서도
반짝반짝 작은 별
아름답게 비치네

Twinkle, Twinkle
Twinkle, twinkle, little star
Lighting beautifully
In the east sky
In the west sky
Twinkle, twinkle, little star
It shines beautifully.

자장가

잘자라 우리아가
앞뜰과 뒷동산에
새들도 아가양도 잠을 자는데
달님은 영창으로
은구슬 금구슬을
보내는 이한밤
잘자라 우리아가 잘 자거라

Lullaby
Sleep well, my baby
In the garden and on the back hill
Birds and lambs are sleeping
The moon brings silver
And gold beads to the dawn
Through the night
Sleep well, my baby, sleep well.

안녕히 주무세요 엄마.
안녕히 주무세요 아빠.
사랑해요.
잘자 친구들아.

Goodnight, Mommy.
Goodnight, Daddy.
I love you.
Goodnight, dear friends.

잘자 친구들아

잘자 친구들아 잘자
잘자 친구들아 잘자
잘자 친구들아
잘자 친구들아
잘자 친구들아 잘자
잘자

Goodnight My Friends
Goodnight, my friends, goodnight
Goodnight, my friends, goodnight
Goodnight, my friends
Goodnight, my friends
Goodnight, my friends, goodnight.
Goodnight!

색깔

빨간색

보라색

파란색

초록색

주황색

회색

노란색

분홍색

고동색

하얀색

검정색